Loose Him and Let Him Go

A Manuel in Deliverance

John Edwards

LOOSE HIM AND LET HIM GO

A MANUAL IN DELIVERANCE

JOHN EDWARDS

Layout and cover design by Guiding Productions
Edited by Stephan Krueger

Published by AwakenMedia.de
Postfach 1132
Ebersbach an der Fils, Germany

ISBN: 978-3-945339-17-6

1st Edition

www.awakenmedia.de

CONTENTS

FOREWORD

This is the book you have been waiting for!
Loose Him and Let Him Go is both a Bible study and a practical manual on deliverance. The truths in God's Word are essentially simple – it is obeying them that we find difficult. The book in your hands will encourage you to act according to the verse ... *"And these signs will accompany those who believe: In my name they will drive out demons"* (Mark 16:17).

For many years Christians have read *"For our struggle is not..."* (Ephesians 6:12) and stopped reading right there. Our fight is against the devil and his demonic spirits not one another in the body of Christ. Deliverance touches every area of our lives. Husbands and wives need to minister deliverance to each other; parents to children; Christians to Christians. Let us shake the kingdom of darkness, tear the demonic ruling princes from their seats of power, *"...proclaim freedom for the prisoners and ... set the oppressed free"* (Luke 4:18).

John has ministered deliverance for over forty years and I have had the privilege of working with him at different

times. What he has written he put into practice and this book is an expression of his desire to see the whole body of Christ ministering deliverance.
Read it and do it!

Malcolm Harland
Open Door Community Church Pastoral Team

THE DELIVERANCE MINISTRY

THE NEED FOR DELIVERANCE

The spirit world is real, in spite of the world's ideas. The Bible, which is of course our basis, teaches that there are angels and demons and that they are active in the lives of men and women (Hebrews 1:14; Ephesians 6:10-12; 1 John 5:19). Did you know that? More to the point, have you been willing to recognize it? The Christian often has a credibility gap – it is one thing to know the theory of what the Word teaches about spiritual realities, and quite another to face up to the fact that our everyday lives and the lives of others we meet are so affected. We need to move out of theory into daily practice. One of the ways the enemy will attack you as you begin to deal with the demonic, is that the thought will come to you, "It's too far-fetched". You see, the devil does not like people getting involved in this ministry. He'll do everything in his power to squeeze you out, frighten you, and cause you to doubt or fear. The more you determine to go on, the greater awareness and certainty you will have about the spirit realm.

Our example is Jesus. He constantly moved in this ministry (Luke 4:18-19; 13:32 [his calling] and Colossians 1:13 [what salvation is]). Those who have personally had spirits cast out will readily appreciate the need for this ministry.

THE CHALLENGE FOR OUR DAY

We are at the end of the age of the outpouring of the Holy Spirit; at the same time there is an upsurge in demonic activity. The challenge is:

- To move with and into new areas of revelation. Truths are being restored.
  "Hear what the Spirit says to the churches." Demons have always been at work, but our understanding has only recently increased – this is one of the many areas being restored, along with worship, faith and spiritual gifts.
- To meet the needs of many who are coming into the Kingdom, whose past lives have been torn apart by Satan. The breakdown of restraints and the social patterns of a Christian heritage have made the inroads of the demonic more noticeable.

WHO SHOULD BE INVOLVED?

We are God's people for our generation; the task is given to us. It is one of the most rewarding works to be involved in. It is a part of the work of ministry that is to be done by the members of the body (Ephesians 4:11-12). This is not a specialized work for the few. Mark 16:17 states: *"And these signs will accom-*

pany those who believe: In my name they will drive out demons". Am I qualified? Are you a believer? If you are saved, you have received the authority to use the name of Jesus – you are qualified. Having said that, you must also have zeal (John 2:17) – presumably you have, or you wouldn't be reading this; knowledge (1 Corinthians 9:26) – that's the purpose of this course; and wisdom (James 1:5) – comes from asking God and through experience.

IN DELIVERANCE, WHAT ARE WE SEEKING TO DO?

- Recognize and expel demon spirits from the bodies of men, women and children. Keep this objective clearly in mind.
- To instruct those set free on how to remain free.
- To give support to those in spiritual conflict. Stay clear of arguments with others who say that it is not possible for Christians to be demonized, and don't try to categorize – oppressed, possessed, compressed, impressed, depressed. In other words, don't waste your time. Avoid phrases that hedge and fudge.

Scriptures to ponder

Finally, be strong in the Lord and in his mighty power. Put on the full armor of God, so that you can take your stand against the devil's schemes. For our struggle is not against flesh and blood, but against the rulers, against the authorities, against the powers of this dark world and against the spiritual forces of evil in the heavenly realms.
(Ephesians 6:10-12)

"The Spirit of the Lord is on me, because he has anointed me to proclaim good news to the poor. He has sent me to proclaim freedom for the prisoners and recovery of sight for the blind, to set the oppressed free, to proclaim the year of the Lord's favor".
(Luke 4:18-19)

For he has rescued us from the dominion of darkness and brought us into the kingdom of the Son he loves.
(Colossians 1:13)

And these signs will accompany those who believe: In my name they will drive out demons; they will speak in new tongues.
(Mark 16:17)

KNOW THAT JESUS IS THE VICTOR

Fill your heart with what the Word says about the total victory of Jesus: Genesis 3:15; Matthew 28:18; Luke 10:18-20; Romans 8:37-39; Philippians 2:9; Colossians 2:14-15; 1 John 4:4 and Revelation 1:17-18.

We cast out demons in the name (i.e. authority) of Jesus and that authority is exercised by faith. Spirits are aware of confidence and assurance – news travels fast on the demonic grapevine (Acts 19:15). The more you move in this area the more confidence you have, and the speedier the results. Some spirits will boast that they are strong and powerful. Some may seem difficult to dislodge, and there will be various reasons for that. But Jesus is the victor – the victory has already been won, and we are simply putting that victory into effect.

KNOW YOUR ENEMY

Never fall into the trap of feeling sorry for demons – at times they whimper and plead. Psalm 139:21-22 – their aim is to torment and destroy. In some ways Satan is very short on ideas (2 Corinthians 2:11 – schemes, settled war plan). In a war, a good general, studies his opponents; not that we seek to obtain a Ph.D. in witchcraft (you'd then need deliverance yourself), but we need to be aware of how demons operate; how the mind is attacked, what spirits to expect to be working together, how they got in and how to recognize them.

KNOW YOUR WEAPONS

The Christian's weapons are the name of Jesus, the blood of Jesus, and the Word of God. We also need the Holy Spirit's discernment, and sometimes he even supplies the words to say. You must be clear about this that we cast out spirits by our words – we don't fight witchcraft with witchcraft! Avoid superstitious ideas for confronting demons such as 'holy water' etc. (Matthew 8:16; 2 Thessalonians 2:8; Revelation 1:16 and 12:11).

At first great difficulty may be experienced in speaking out loud to demons, especially when they do not respond – this is pressure from the enemy. It is very effective to quote scripture – Jesus did when tempted by the devil (Matthew 4:1-11).

It is also good to magnify and praise Jesus and even to sing (be open to the Holy Spirit's leading). Tell the spirits what Jesus has done and what their end is. Quote scriptures that are against the particular activity of the spirit you are dealing with. For example, if you are up against a spirit of hatred, you might say, *"This person loves Jesus, for the love of God has been shed abroad in his heart"* (Romans 5:5).

WE ARE PART OF A BODY

Work with someone else; Jesus sent his disciples out two by two. Know your weaknesses and limitations. Don't let Satan get you on the runaround, and when you are over tired. Call in help, pass on those you can't cope with, and learn from others.

KEEP YOURSELF RIGHT

Being in the deliverance ministry means that you will be a target for the enemy, but because you are involved, you will get greater protection (Luke 22:31). In addition, the more you pray for others and learn how spirits get a hold on people, the more aware you will become of his schemes and traps.

HOW DO I START?

The Biblical principle is that disciples learn directly from a master e.g. Elisha and Elijah, Samuel and Eli, and of course the disciples and the Lord. Ask the Lord for opportunities and openings to accompany someone more experienced than you.

Scriptures to ponder

Then Jesus came to them and said, 'All authority in heaven and on earth has been given to me'.
(Matthew 28:18)

He replied, 'I saw Satan fall like lightning from heaven. I have given you authority to trample on snakes and scorpions and to overcome all the power of the enemy; nothing will harm you. However, do not rejoice that the spirits submit to you, but rejoice that your names are written in heaven'.
(Luke 10:18-20)

Having canceled the charge of our legal indebtedness, which stood against us and condemned us; he has taken it away, nailing it to the cross. And having disarmed the powers and authorities, he made a public spectacle of them, triumphing over them by the cross.
(Colossians 2:14-15)

You, dear children, are from God and have overcome them, because the one who is in you is greater than the one who is in the world.
(1 John 4:4)

UNDERSTAND WHAT DEMONS ARE

WHAT ARE DEMONS?

Demons are spirits without bodies who seek bodies to operate in and through in their desire to fight against God and those whom God loves. They are not fallen angels, who have bodies. Their origin is a matter of speculation. Possibly therefore they are a pre-Adamic race, or a product of the sons of God and daughters of men (Genesis 6:1-2). They certainly prefer to dwell in a human body (Matthew 12:43-45), but will at times enter bodies of animals (Mark 5:11-13).

They have all the normal marks of personality:

Will	Choice and preference (Matthew 12:44; Mark 5:12).
Emotion	Shudder, apprehension and fear (James 2:19).
Knowledge	"I know who you are" (Mark 1:23-24; Acts 19:15).
Self-awareness	"My name is Legion" (Mark 5:9).

A conscience	Though too seared to respond (1 Tim 4:1-2).
Ability to speak	Mark 1:23-24; Mark 5:7-12; Acts 19:15.

SATAN'S FORCES ARE LIKE AN ARMY

Satan's forces are structured like an army with various ranks and powers (Ephesians 6:12). When Satan fell he drew down with him a number of the spiritual intelligences, which God had appointed to assist him in his government. Part of Satan's hierarchy consists of these fallen angels – possibly a third of the original angelic host (Revelation 12:3-4; 7-9). Angels have bodies and do not seek human bodies to live in. Indeed they are of a higher order than us. In deliverance, we are dealing with demons, not angels.

DIFFERENT KINDS OF DEMONS

There are different kinds of demons; they are not all the same. In Matthew 12:45, Jesus refers to spirits that are 'more evil' than others and in Mark 9:29, he speaks of 'this kind' thus distinguishing the spirit he is dealing with from other kinds that may be encountered. But whatever spirits you do come up against, be sure that they are demons, you won't encounter Satan himself! Sometimes they say "I am Satan" or "I am Lucifer" but that is only to frighten you. In John 13:27 it says that Satan entered into Judas, but this was probably only a manner of speaking – he entered through the agency of demons. This is parallel to the case of a Christian;

it is said that both the Father and Jesus will dwell in him (John 14:23), and they do so, but only in the sense that the Holy Spirit, whom they are one with, dwells in us. Satan is the prince of the power of the air with his power base in the heavenlies.

ACTIVITY OF DEMONS

Outside the body – influence
In this instance, they need only to be resisted (James 4:7; 1 Peter 5:8-9).

Within the body – control
In this case they need to be expelled, driven out.

Scriptures to ponder

When an impure spirit comes out of a person, it goes through arid places seeking rest and does not find it. Then it says, 'I will return to the house I left.' When it arrives, it finds the house unoccupied, swept clean and put in order. Then it goes and takes with it seven other spirits more wicked than itself, and they go in and live there. And the final condition of that person is worse than the first. That is how it will be with this wicked generation.
(Matthew 12:43-45)

Just then a man in their synagogue who was possessed by an impure spirit cried out, "What do you want with us, Jesus of Nazareth? Have you come to destroy us? I know who you are – the Holy One of God!"
(Mark 1:23-24)

Then war broke out in heaven. Michael and his angels fought against the dragon, and the dragon and his angels fought back. But he was not strong enough, and they lost their place in heaven. The great dragon was hurled down – that ancient serpent called the devil, or Satan, who leads the whole world astray. He was hurled to the earth, and his angels with him.
(Revelation 12:7-9)

Submit yourselves, then, to God. Resist the devil, and he will flee from you.
(James 4:7)

WHAT DEMONS SEEK TO DO

1. Entice – they tempt people to sin with suggestions to the mind; "take it, no-one will know." Children are often subject to this. The Lord was tempted by suggestions (Matthew 4:1-11).

2. Deceive – by demons, Satan deceives and blinds people to the truth (2 Corinthians 4:4) and even takes away the word that was sown in them (Mark 4:15).

3. Enslave – there is a spirit of slavery (Romans 8:15), by which Satan holds people in chains, forcing men and women to do his will. Many are not aware that they are slaves until they seek to do what the Lord wants, and then they realize that they are enslaved to habits, cravings and unclean desires, or to drink and do drugs, or to depression and fear.

4. Torment – they delight in causing anguish and pain, physical, mental and emotional – fear has torment.

5. Compel – Compulsion is a classic sign of demonization (Luke 8:29). Perfectionism (often the case with sports enthusiasts), restlessness and suicide are manifestations of this. It takes away peace and breaks down harmony, physically, in relationships and with regard to circumstances.

6. Defile – They seek to debase what God intended as a temple of the Holy Spirit – demons are at the root of all perversion (Romans 1:21-32). All forms of sexual immorality open doors to evil spirits, who then promote the uncleanness that let them in (1 Corinthians 6:18-20). They seek to ruin men and women morally, spiritually, physically and mentally, since whatever God loves, Satan hates.

HOW TO TELL IF SOMEONE NEEDS DELIVERANCE

If you are going to minister deliverance, this is obviously an important question. There are two ways of knowing:

1. By Revelation

One of the gifts of the Holy Spirit is the discerning of spirits, whereby the indwelling Holy Spirit discloses to you the spirit in a person. Some people see spirits, others hear them in the spirit, but more common is a word of knowledge given by the Holy Spirit.

2. By Detection

When someone comes with problems and difficulties, as they talk you become aware of the spirits by way of the symptoms – just as a doctor will diagnose a physical problem:

PROBLEMS THAT SUGGEST THE PRESENCE OF A DEMON

- Emotional – resentment, rejection, self-pity, hatred, anger, jealousy, depression, worry, inferiority, insecurity, fear.
- Mental – torment, indecision, compromise, doubt, confusion, rationalization, loss of memory.
- Speech – lying, cursing, blasphemy, criticism, mockery, railing, gossip.
- Sexual – unclean acts and thoughts, fantasy, sex experience, masturbation, perversions, adultery, homosexuality, lust, incest, fornication, harlotry and provocativeness.
- Addiction – nicotine, alcohol, drugs, medicines, caffeine, food.
- Physical – allergies, migraine, skin disorders, cancers. Often prayer for healing is needed afterwards.
- Religious error – false religions, Christian cults, occult, false doctrines.

Find out the areas they have already had deliverance in; it is good to talk and ask a few questions since demons tend to show off and give themselves away.

A good counselor listens sympathetically, yet at the same time, beware of self-pity and being emotionally pressurized.

DEMONS OPERATE IN GROUPS

This is because the entrance of one spirit will open the door to others (Matthew 12:45). In groups there is often a dominant or ruling spirit. Example of a group: resentment, hatred, bitterness, anger, violence and murder (the names of demons relate to their nature).

THERE IS A PROGRESSION OF CONTROL

A good example is Saul in the Old Testament, 1 Samuel chapters 18-30. From being initially depressed (music was called for to uplift him), he went steadily downhill into jealousy, anger, rage, hatred, murder, fear, paranoia, occult involvement and suicide. During all this, notice the swings in his attitude to David (1 Samuel 19:10-11; 24:16-17; 26:21).

THE ATTITUDE OF THE PERSON

The person who needs deliverance can hinder or help in deliverance by his attitude – his co-operation is vital, he must be willing to submit to your ministry (this will be dealt with more fully later). So far we have considered the case of someone who has come to you for deliverance, knowing that they need it; but what about the person who is unaware of his need of ministry? Do you tell them that they need it?

No hard-and-fast rule can be made, since it depends on the person, your relationship with them, and the way it is done. Be open to the Holy Spirit's leading. A personal testimony as to how the Lord delivered you is a good way of introducing the subject and encouraging others.

Scriptures to ponder

Some people are like seed along the path, where the word is sown. As soon as they hear it, Satan comes and takes away the word that was sown in them.
(Mark 4:15)

The Spirit you received does not make you slaves, so that you live in fear again; rather, the Spirit you received brought about your adoption to sonship. And by him we cry, "Abba, Father."
(Romans 8:15)

For Jesus had commanded the impure spirit to come out of the man. Many times it had seized him, and though he was chained hand and foot and kept under guard, he had broken his chains and had been driven by the demon into solitary places.
(Luke 8:29)

Flee from sexual immorality. All other sins a person commits are outside the body, but whoever sins sexually, sins against their own body. Do you not know that your bodies are temples of the Holy Spirit, who is in you, whom you have received from God? You are not your own; you were bought at a price. Therefore honor God with your bodies.
(1 Corinthians 6:18-20)

HOW DEMONS ENTER

HOW DEMONS ENTER

How do these evil personalities get inside? Jesus gave us the analogy of our bodies being a house; they get in if a door is opened to them (Matthew 12:44-45). Man was made in the image of God and so structured physically, emotionally and psychologically as to be a dwelling place for God's Spirit (1 Corinthians 3:16; 2 Corinthians 6:16). But this means he can also be a dwelling place for evil spirits, for his "house" is difficult to keep empty. There is a lesson for us in the Temple of Jerusalem (Matthew 21:12-13). Designed as a house for God's presence it had become a den of thieves that needed cleansing by Jesus.

Demons cannot walk in and out as they please for God made us with a natural defense. Even the unsaved have a natural resistance to demons gaining entrance. What, then, opens the door? Primarily, sin lets demons in. Contrast Genesis 4:6-7 with Revelation 3:20. The demon will spring in through the open door – Jesus waits for an invitation. Thus we are warned in Proverbs 4:23: *Above all else, guard your heart, for everything you do flows from it.*

1. SIN – sin opens the door to demons. The story of Ananias and Sapphira (Acts 5:1-11) is very instructive. They agreed to lie and deceive; *Satan has so filled your heart* (vs. 3). As they gave way to lying, covetousness and deceit, demons were able to control them.

In Galatians 5:19-21 the acts of the sinful nature are listed. *Sexual immorality impurity and debauchery; idolatry and witchcraft; hatred, discord, jealousy, fits of rage, selfish ambition, dissensions, factions and envy, drunkenness, orgies, and the like.* There are demons who correspond to all such acts and if a person persistently yields to the sins of the flesh he opens a door for demons to come in. We are to crucify the flesh, i.e. say no to sin and refuse to gratify evil desires, and thus give no ground to the enemy. Part of the work of ministering deliverance is to teach the need of crucifying the flesh, and through discipline to keep the door shut (Romans 6:16-19; Job 31:1). We must teach people about the dangers of loving money (1 Timothy 6:9-10; 1 John 2:16). Judas fell through lying and theft. If we do not guard ourselves we will be in trouble.

2. CIRCUMSTANCES OF LIFE - adverse circumstances can reduce our natural resistance to demons by our being weakened physically, emotionally or mentally. Times of crisis can always be dangerous, but particularly so in childhood; upset in the home, anger, and violence between parents, separation, broken homes, being attacked or abused, or simply not feeling loved or accepted, can all open the door. Earlier still, the trauma of a difficult birth can have its effect. Times of physical weakness can be dangerous, too. Sickness, lack of food and sleep deprivation can all leave their mark. Women after giving birth can be in danger, perhaps not so much in allowing a spirit to enter as giving more ground to one already there. Accidents can let in the spirit of death and fear of accidents; indeed any shock or sudden fear can allow the enemy in – nightmares, films that cause fear, asthma attacks etc. (shell-shock suffered during the First World War is a good example of emotional trauma letting demons in). Children should be particularly protected from emotional trauma that would make them vulnerable – it is good to pray with a child immediately when there's been a sudden shock or fear.

3. WRONG THINKING – In Philippians 4:8, Paul counsels us to think on good things, precisely because the opposite, wrong thinking can be dangerous. Negative thoughts, rebellion, resentment, fantasy, day-dreaming, unclean thoughts and anger (Ephesians 4:26) – are all to be guarded against, and if necessary dealt with (2 Corinthians 10:5). Wrong thinking will inevitably lead to wrong speaking, and such things as hopelessness, unbelief and doubt can be detected by listening to people's words – they will say "it's no use" or "nothing can be done" or similar.

4. FALSE RELIGIONS – Idol worship is demon worship, and involvement with false religions lets demons in. Roman Catholics' worship of Mary and the saints, the burning of incense and the use of rosary beads, can open the door, too. Often the very possession of religious articles can hinder deliverance.

5. OCCULT – False religions and the occult often overlap. The basic meaning of the word 'occult' is hidden or obscured. It covers all fortune telling, magic practices, spiritism, all attempts to gain knowledge, power and abilities outside of what God has decreed permissible. There is a flood of occult practice today in Britain, Europe and the USA. God's Word makes it very clear that all occult practices are forbidden (Deuteronomy 18:9-14; Leviticus 19:26-31; 20:6.27; Exodus 22:18; Revelation 21:8). Often you will have to point out that it is wrong, so have these scriptures already marked in your Bible to turn to, and then you will have to be able to spell out what these practices are in today's terms. Occult practices often found today: Ouija board, horoscope, meditation, automatic writing, water divining, ESP, telepathy, charming away illness, faith healing, yoga, hypnosis, tarot cards, acupuncture and superstition. This list is not exhaustive. There's no such thing as white and black magic – it's all black.

There is a tendency in the fallen nature of man to seek the supernatural through occult practices, which exert a real fascination for the mind. But the occult always brings depression and confusion, as well as obvious moral evil. Ecclesiastes 10:8 tells us that God has set the limits, with his Word as a wall or hedge which we may not break through without opening ourselves up to demonization.

6. DRUGS AND ALCOHOL – By taking away a person's self-control, drugs and alcohol are a direct opening for demons (Proverbs 25:28). Even prescribed drugs can have this effect. Praying for someone on drugs can be especially difficult as it often neutralizes the person's will so that the demons have a tighter hold. Often drugs prescribed for psychiatric disorders seem to cut a person off from being aware of the manifestation of the demon and from the feeling of release as it leaves.

7. INHERITANCE – Spirits can be passed down from one generation to another, with a curse upon disobedience (Exodus 20:4-5; Deuteronomy 28:15; Jeremiah 31:29). Occult involvement, sickness, sexual sin, alcoholism, Freemasonry and illegitimacy are all things that are likely to hand down evil effects, in many cases with the same pattern of life being repeated: the curse gives the demon the right to enter. However, Christ has redeemed us from the curse and can break this chain of evil effects by casting the demons out (Galatians 3:13-14).

DOES IT MATTER HOW THEY GET IN?

It matters in as much as it can help those delivered to shut the door in the future. Revelation often comes to those praying or to the person receiving deliverance, as to how and when that demon came in; the latter may remember an incident or feel certain emotions or sensations that they recognize from the past.

Scriptures to ponder

Don't you know that you yourselves are God's temple and that God's Spirit dwells in your midst?
(1 Corinthians 3:16)

Finally, brothers and sisters, whatever is true, whatever is noble, whatever is right, whatever is pure, whatever is lovely, whatever is admirable – if anything is excellent or praiseworthy – think about such things.
(Philippians 4:8)

The weapons we fight with are not the weapons of the world. On the contrary, they have divine power to demolish strongholds. We demolish arguments and every pretension that sets itself up against the knowledge of God, and we take captive every thought to make it obedient to Christ.
(2 Corinthians 10:4-5)

But the cowardly, the unbelieving, the vile, the murderers, the sexually immoral, those who practice magic arts, the idolaters and all liars – they will be consigned to the fiery lake of burning sulfur. This is the second death.
(Revelation 21:8)

HOW TO EXPEL DEMONS

HOW TO GET DEMONS OUT

There is only one way to deal with demons and that is the Bible's way – the only hope we have is the victory Jesus won for us.

1. The Person Needing Deliverance

- Must have confidence in the power of Jesus. Faith comes by God's Word. We're to encourage all to believe what the Lord can do – no demon is too strong for Jesus – so show them from the Bible examples of God's mighty deliverance. Don't tell people how difficult it is to be free, the demons will have already told them that; don't be like others who feel it's their task in life to persuade people that they're not saved!

- Must have confidence in you. The demons know if you're operating in faith. If the person being ministered to won't accept your ministry, it's a waste of time to continue. Co-operation is important.

- Must be honest. They must be honest with themselves, with God and with those ministering. Demons thrive in darkness. Pride or fear often keeps people from being open, but the Lord knows all about us. Many fear disgrace and being thought of as terrible, and also fear that their problem will become widely known. You must give assurance that their problems are by no means unique, and anyway that what they have shared will be kept in strictest confidence.

  The Lord can and does indeed give revelation through a word of knowledge, but a person who says "If the Lord wants you to know, he'll tell you himself" is avoiding the issue. Why should the Lord disclose it when the person could? Very often it is sexual sins that people are fearful of sharing, but that is to fall into Satan's trap – he knows that confession is part of the answer, and he tries to deter us from it (Psalms 32:5; 139:23-24; Proverbs 28:13). Sometimes a person will need encouragement to confess, and reassurance afterwards.

- Humility. A recognition of our dependence upon the Lord and his grace is vital (James 4:6-7). This will show itself in the response of the person needing help to those who seek to minister.

- Repentance. Since it's nearly always sin that has opened the door to demons, repentance – being determined to turn away from sin – is necessary to close it again. This is vital for certain demons – of violence, hatred, sexual sins and occult practices. The person seeking freedom must come out of agreement with those activities and thoughts.

At times it will be necessary to show why something is wrong, and also to explain the nature of repentance, that it is an act of the will, a determination to walk God's way. You must make it clear that we are not ruled by emotions or pressures, that God have given us the ability to choose.

- Renunciation. Renunciation is what is said and done as an evidence of repentance. To speak out and say 'I renounce' this or that activity can be a trigger in deliverance. Some have great difficulty in saying it – they have a physical struggle to do so. A person can be hesitant and even confused as to whether they really do want to stop doing a certain thing, and it is renouncing it that breaks the bondage.

  Actions evidencing repentance are the destroying of books, emblems, charms or drugs (Matthew 3:7-8; Acts 19:18-19).

- Forgiveness. It is always good to emphasize the need to forgive; ask if there are any who have caused hurt and ask about the willingness to forgive, explaining that it's an act of the will, like repentance. Get them to say that they forgive, and name the person in a prayer; often it is good to lead the person in prayer (Matthew 6:14-15).

- Prayer. Encourage the person to ask God to set them free, before you actually get down to the deliverance itself (Joel 2:32; Psalms 145:19).

2. Those Ministering

- Recognize the authority we have in the name of Jesus. All authority in heaven and earth has been given to Jesus, and he ministers it through us (Matthew 28:18; Mark 16:17). It's a serious business, but don't get too intense. It's good to operate in teams or as couples. It is good for the person receiving deliverance to know what you intend to do, and also what to expect.

- Prayer is directed towards God, warfare towards the enemy. Identify the spirits and command them to leave in the name of Jesus, speaking directly to them. Our weapons are the blood of Jesus and the word of God (Ephesians 6:17; James 4:7; Revelation 12:11).

DEMONS GENERALLY LEAVE BY THE MOUTH

The Greek word *pneuma* means spirit, breath and wind (it is translated wind in John 3:8), as does the Hebrew word *ruach*, so it is not surprising that demons should leave by the mouth. At one point the demon will be inside, and then it will leave – that's what we're aiming at, the expulsion of the spirits. Sometimes those seeking deliverance can help in the process of expulsion, and should be encouraged to do so; on many occasions no such encouragement will be needed – the person may be gasping, choking, yawning, belching, sighing, screaming, whining, whimpering, retching or sobbing.

At times when such manifestations are not forthcoming, a positive action of expelling will help, such as breathing out or coughing. You have to balance the encouragement you give people to do this with the criticism that will come that this is just auto-suggestion. Of course we are concerned not to let the ministry of deliverance fall into disrepute by unwise actions, but whatever you do Satan will seek to ridicule and cause criticism. Since the important thing is to get the person in need free, it's sometimes necessary to risk criticism to help the afflicted.

KEEP YOUR EYES OPEN

As you minister, watch what takes place. At times you will see the reaction of demons in the expression on the person's face, or in the movements of the body. The person may be aware of the reaction – it may be violent – but not always. Demons will try to remain undetected, but the power and authority of the Holy Spirit will force them out into the open. It is good to ask people if they can feel anything while being ministered to, because physical reaction becomes something tangible, showing that they are getting to grips with the enemy. So it can bean encouragement to their faith and confidence. Make the point that the reason the demon reacts is because it has to yield.

When you first start to minister, Satan will try to put you off, frighten you, bring you into criticism or ridicule, or simply try to make nothing happen. If you pray for people while others who are skeptical are present, it may be that nothing happens. Their unbelief doesn't help, and the enemy doesn't want them enlightened. Jesus sometimes asked people to leave when he was about to minister, because he did not want to operate in an atmosphere of unbelief (Mark 5:39-43).

Scriptures to ponder

Then I acknowledged my sin to you and did not cover up my iniquity. I said, "I will confess my transgressions to the Lord."
(Psalms 32:5)

For if you forgive other people when they sin against you, your heavenly Father will also forgive you. But if you do not forgive others their sins, your Father will not forgive your sins.
(Matthew 6:14-15)

And these signs will accompany those who believe: In my name they will drive out demons.
(Mark 16:17)

They triumphed over him by the blood of the Lamb and by the word of their testimony; they did not love their lives so much as to shrink from death.
(Revelation 12:11)

INDIVIDUAL TECHNIQUES

As in many other ministries, people develop their own way of operating. As long as it is in line with scripture that's fine, but don't let people tell you that their way is the proper way with a whole list of rules and techniques. Some people have strange ideas about deliverance; e.g. the person must kneel, make the sign of the cross, take bread and wine before, or apply oil afterwards. We must beware of superstitions.

NORMAL PROCEDURE

1. Encourage the person seeking deliverance to relax.
2. Ask about the problems or the need.
3. Say something about what deliverance is, and the victory being ours only through Jesus. Be wise and don't frighten the person.
4. Satisfy yourself that the person is saved, if not lead them in a prayer for salvation. If not sure, do it anyway.
5. Encourage the person to talk about himself/herself (demons often give themselves away by boasting), putting in a question from time-to-time if you need to (ask about trauma, childhood fears etc).

6. Write down what you will probably have to deal with.
7. Mention the requirements for getting free.
8. Explain what you are going to do in a positive fashion, making it not too lengthy or complicated.
9. Encourage the person to pray.
10. Bind demons outside if necessary (the demons in the person may be drawing strength from objects in the room).
11. Begin to speak directly to the demons, commanding them to go in the name of Jesus. Be open to the guidance of the Holy Spirit.

Laying on hands at times can help. You don't need to shout. At times there is a boldness that is more impassioned that comes from an anointing. From time-to-time give encouragement. Even if a spirit manifests strongly and begins to talk, the person generally can still hear you and co-operate with you. Since the aim is to get the demons out as quickly as possible, don't get taken up with their antics. And don't be intimidated by them, should they threaten you; "I'll get you, I know your secret" or "I'll get your family".

DO'S AND DON'TS FOR DELIVERANCE MINISTERS

1. Don't use pat answers: "I know just how you feel", "Just trust in the Lord" or "Just give it all to Jesus".
2. Don't think you must have an instant answer for everything. If you don't have an answer, don't make one up. It's all right to say you don't know, but try to find out.

3. Don't feel responsible to cast out every demon you can in one session. The person can only keep out so many demons. They must battle to keep whatever ground they have gained.
4. Don't wear yourself out, or the person being ministered to. Limit personal sessions to about two hours.
5. Don't become a permanent crutch. Teach the person to stand in their own faith, practice self-deliverance and to discipline their life.
6. Don't give advice contrary to scripture.
7. Don't advise a person to presume on God e.g. to throw away his medications. Let him proceed at the level of his own faith.
8. Don't discuss the person's case with others without their permission.
9. Don't minister alone in private with someone of the opposite sex. In every situation do your best to have another person with you. Jesus sent out his disciples two by two.
10. Do be very careful about physical contact.
11. Don't be sloppy; in the way you counsel, personal appearance, body odor, bad breath.
12. Don't minister when tired: be rested.
13. Don't think you can't fail or make a mistake (1 Corinthians 10:12; 1 Timothy 3:6). Don't become proud.
14. Don't interrogate demons. Develop the gifts of the Holy Spirit, especially discerning of spirits and the word of knowledge.
15. Don't resort to fleshly methods.

VARIOUS MANIFESTATIONS

The same sorts of demons tend to manifest in the same way; but this is a guide not a rule, for they are deceivers. Often the manifestations will give you an idea of what demons you are dealing with. In the USA, Germany and Spain we have seen the same manifestations in people who know nothing of deliverance. Some of the manifestations that are often seen affect the eyes, tongue, hands, feet and legs. The following list may prove helpful but should be taken as a guide only.

- **Mocking laugh** – witchcraft
- **Cramped hands and fingers** – lust
- **Pins and needles in hands** – masturbation
- **Sensations in upper legs** – adultery
- **Deathly look** – death
- **Buzzing in head** – occult etc.

Often the expression on the person's face will remind you of something, and give a clue as to the spirit there. Generally you can take it that when the manifestation is finished, the demon is out. At times it needs perseverance. If there seems to be a blockage, take a break – talk to the person, and look for something that is stopping the person getting free.

BLOCKS TO DELIVERANCE

Unforgiveness, involvement in the occult, involvement in cults, abortion, unconfessed adultery, various idols, non co-operation, resentment, fear, rebellion. Know when to stop. We give the lead, not the demons, so don't be pressured into going on when you feel you should stop. Counsel and advise afterwards.

Scriptures to ponder

So, if you think you are standing firm, be careful that you don't fall!
(1 Corinthians 10:12)

"When an impure spirit comes out of a person, it goes through arid places seeking rest and does not find it. Then it says, 'I will return to the house I left.' When it arrives, it finds the house unoccupied, swept clean and put in order. Then it goes and takes with it seven other spirits more wicked than itself, and they go in and live there. And the final condition of that person is worse than the first. That is how it will be with this wicked generation."
(Matthew 12:43-45)

HOW TO KEEP FREE

KEEPING FREE

Having ministered deliverance, bring your time to a close. Don't be under pressure – the person ministering (while remaining sensitive to the Holy Spirit) is the one in charge.

REASSURANCE

The person who has received ministry may feel shocked at what has happened, but that reaction will soon pass. Don't let them think that they are a weird or terrible case – let them know that they are quite normal, and seek to prevent embarrassment. After ministry, a time of worship and thanksgiving is good, the one delivered being encouraged to pray. If the person has not received the infilling of the Holy Spirit and is open, this is often a good time to pray for them as the demons that were a block to receiving have gone. Have a cup of coffee together if there is time.

MOPPING UP

As the encouragement of a chat develops, something may be said that prompts the thought that there may be more to deal with; demons are boasters and even at this stage may give themselves away with a remark such as "I don't think I can cope with this". So deliverance may continue later.

A PROCESS

Deliverance is a process that often continues over a period of months – seek to make that clear. Point out that self-deliverance is possible, and at the same time tell them not to be afraid to ask for further help. Encourage a positive attitude. Common questions are "I want to know they're all gone" and "Am I totally free?". The only way you can answer is "So do I", and "I don't know"; to tell someone that they are totally free is to go beyond what you know unless you have special discernment and leading. That someone should be able to say "So-and-so told me I've got no demons in me", would only cause problems. If you asked a doctor about your health, he could only reply with honesty, "As far as I know, you have nothing wrong".

EMPHASIZE THE NEED TO STAY FREE

Demons will try to return (Matthew 12:43-45). Some know this scripture and it panics them – that's the ex-

treme reaction you need to guard against, and strike a balance between fear of demons and careless living.
Along with recognition of the reality of the demonic there needs to be knowledge of how to keep free – how to 'live above the snake line' as Frank Hammond puts it.
So new is the realization of the demonic to some that there is a natural overreaction – the parallel with children learning about germs at school who then wash their hands dozens of times a day until they settle down with this truth.

FOLLOW-UP IMPORTANT

Follow-up is always important, and for some it's vital – their pattern of thinking and personal habits and life-style need to undergo a dramatic change. Give counsel, bearing in mind the demons that have been cast out. For example, if the spirits of anger and hatred have been dealt with, your counsel should be to guard against the thought-life, so as to give "no opportunity to the devil" (Ephesians 4:26-27). Also, encourage the person to cultivate the fruit of the Spirit that is opposite in nature, in this case love. They also need to be on guard against counter attack – things go well for a while and then a rebuff comes along, and they must be careful not to let the spirit back in again e.g. rejection, temptation with alcohol.

Follow-up of those within your own fellowship is obviously easier than those from outside. You must realize that your ministry may not always be welcomed by those in other churches – they don't like the idea that they haven't got all the answers and necessary ministry. Some will look to deliverance as a cure-all, which it is not; its part of a Christ-centered process of healing, restoration and growth. On the other hand, some will be looking for any excuse to knock deliverance. You seek to help their most hopeless case that they've given up on, and because there is not an instant transformation, that's deliverance, proved useless as far as they are concerned. Some people will need ministry again and again, for often the same spirits get back in. Don't let frustration or impatience guide you, let the Lord show you how to persevere.

SHARING

Encourage the person who has been delivered to be open in sharing what the Lord has done, it's not a guilty secret (Mark 5:18-20). However, this must be done with wisdom; don't cast your pearls before swine (Christians who are against deliverance, the unsaved who would mock and ridicule), and when it is right to share, be careful about disclosing what you were set free from if it would shock or scandalize (Ephesians 5,3.12).

KEEPING FREE

1. Live by the scriptures. This is done by an act of choice.
2. Learn to praise God continually, even when it's difficult – it's not hypocritical to praise when you don't feel like it, God is worthy of it always, regardless of your feelings.

3. Protect and guard your thought life, learn to change thoughts and repent quickly.
4. Cultivate right relationships.
5. Submit to discipline, both in the church and at home.
6. Don't be afraid to spell out what these guidelines mean – some people will need to be told of a specific application of these principles to their situation. Tell them that they should stop going here or there or seeing such-and-such a person.

GUARD YOUR OWN LIFE AND FAMILY

People involved in this ministry need to guard themselves, as well as those who've been ministered to. Watch for these signs: losing your joy; getting overtired; getting too involved with a particular need; pride. Beware of thinking that you are the only one who has the necessary gift or insight to deal with a person or problem.

Scriptures to ponder

"In your anger do not sin": Do not let the sun go down while you are still angry, and do not give the devil a foothold.
(Ephesians 4:26-27)

As Jesus was getting into the boat, the man who had been demon-possessed begged to go with him. Jesus did not let him, but said, "Go home to your own people and tell them how much the Lord has done for you, and how he has had mercy on you." So the man went away and began to tell in the Decapolis how much Jesus had done for him. And all the people were amazed.
(Mark 5:18-20)

But among you there must not be even a hint of sexual immorality, or of any kind of impurity, or of greed, because these are improper for God's holy people. Nor should there be obscenity, foolish talk or coarse joking, which are out of place, but rather thanksgiving.
(Ephesians 5:3-4)

ABOUT JOHN EDWARDS

For over 40 years *John Edwards* was the pastor of *New Life Christian Center Croydon* in South London. Under his leadership, the church grew from a small community of forty Christians to well over a thousand members. John is a sought-after Bible teacher who has taught on spiritual warfare and deliverance across Europe. One of his desires is to see believers equipped to minister deliverance in the context of the local church.

John is married and has seven children. Together with his wife Doris, they have taken in and cared for more than one hundred and fifty foster children over the years.

Johann Christoph Blumhardt

JESUS IS VICTOR!

Blumhardt's Battle with the Powers of Darkness

Forwords by Kevin Dedmon & Walter Heidenreich

More gripping than Frank E. Peretti and Stephen King, this book written by Johann Christoph Blumhardt in 1844 is not a novel, but an enthralling eye-witness account sent to the Senior Church Authorities of the Kingdom of Württemberg. The consequence of the events described was a powerful revival in which the whole village of Möttlingen, with only a few exceptions, was converted. A movement sprang up in which thousands of people were healed from physical sickness and released from spiritual bondage. The lame could walk, the blind could see and bread was multiplied. Even the King of Württemberg paid an anonymous visit to one of the Sunday services which often attracted up to two thousand people to the small country church in Möttlingen. In 1852 the Blumhardts moved as a family to Bad Boll, where they established a healing community to which people from all over Europe were drawn. Blumhardt concluded that the in-breaking of the kingdom of God he had experienced in

Möttlingen represented what Jesus had in store for the whole cosmos. Johann Christoph Blumhardt and his son Christoph Friedrich Blumhardt had a major influence on Theologians such as Karl Barth, Emil Brunner, Dietrich Bonhoeffer and Jürgen Moltmann.

Paperback, 100 pages

US $12.95

NOTES

www.ingramcontent.com/pod-product-compliance
Ingram Content Group UK Ltd.
Pitfield, Milton Keynes, MK11 3LW, UK
UKHW042000190726
13854UKWH00005B/2093

9 783945 339176